D1278070

A Cat Named CAKE

By Cason Rome

Warmest thanks to my closest friends, for they are
my biggest cheerleaders and the reason I still pursue
my artistic dreams. And to my wonderful parents,
because without them I never would have found the
courage to break out of my comfort zone and
finally put my thoughts and ideas on paper.
Through their love and support, I have become
the woman I am today.

– C.R.

MacLaren-Cochrane Publishing, Inc.
Text©2021 Cason Rome
Cover and Interior Art©2021 Cason Rome

A Cat Named Cake Dyslexic Edition

All rights reserved, including the right to
reproduce this book or portions thereof
in any form whatsoever.
For information, e-mail the publisher at:

MCPInfo@Maclaren-Cochranepublishing.com

Library of Congress Control Number: 2021938182

First Edition

ISBN
Hardcover: 978-1-64372-515-4
Softcover: 978-1-64372-514-7

For orders, visit

www.MCP-Store.com
www.maclaren-cochranepublishing.com
www.facebook.com/maclaren-cochranepublishing

Chocolates and Pearls is a very special Shop.

People come from far away for sweet treats to eat!

They have handmade chocolates, marshmallows, and pastries in all shapes, sizes, and flavors.

This is a very special shop indeed!

And in the shop lives a cat.

Not just any cat, a very special cat.
A cat named **C**ake.

Cake has an important job in this
Sweet Shop. She is the Shop's
special night guard!

However, her job isn't to keep people out, no, no!

Her job is to keep all the wonderful sweets inside!

Every night, when the owner locks up the shop, Cake stands guard.

She watches as the Truffles
sprout their little legs...

... and the **C**upcakes rise up from their colorful cups.

She smiles as the Marshmallows puff up behind the glass, trying to escape!

But Cake watches closely, so no one gets out!

She meows in warning at the sweets,
guarding the door with a keen eye...

Oh no!

The Macarons are out of their box again!

She chases them around the display and under the tables.

Cake needs to catch them all!

She chases them into the kitchen...

and over the counters.

Finally, she carefully rolls the cookies back into their box. Whew!! Good job Cake!

The sun is coming up, and Cake can see it
through the shop window.

The night is almost over, and it is time
for the sweets to go back to sleep!

Cake did a good job.
No sweets got away!

Cake's owner is very proud of her
and gives her a treat.

Time for **C**ake to take a break. **S**he has earned a cat nap!

Sleep tight, Cake. Remember, you have a job to do tonight! We're counting on you!

The End

What is Dyslexie Font?

Each letter is given its own identity making it easier for people with dyslexia to be more successful at reading.

The Dyslexia font:

1 Makes letters easier to distinguish
2 Offers more ease, regularity and joy in reading
3 Enables you to read with less effort
4 Gives your self-esteem a boost
5 Can be used anywhere, anytime and on (almost) every device
6 Does not require additional software or programs
7 Offers the simplest and most effective reading support

The Dyslexia font is specially designed for people with dyslexia, in order to make reading easier - and more fun. During the design process, all basic typography rules and standards were ignored. Readability and specific characteristics of dyslexia are used as guidelines for the design.

Graphic designer Christian Boer created a dyslexic-friendly font to make reading easier for people with dyslexia, like himself.

"Traditional fonts are designed solely from an aesthetic point of view," Boer writes on his website, *"which means they often have characteristics that make characters difficult to recognize for people with dyslexia. Oftentimes, the letters of a word are confused, turned around or jumbled up because they look too similar."*

Designed to make reading clearer and more enjoyable for people with dyslexia, Dyslexie uses heavy base lines, alternating stick and tail lengths, larger openings, and semicursive slants to ensure that each character has a unique and more easily recognizable form.

Our books are not just for children to enjoy, they are also for adults that have dyslexia that want the experience of reading to the children in their lives.

Learn more and get the font for your digital devices at www.dyslexiefont.com

Get books in Dyslexie Font at: www.mcp-store.com

3	Hold my Hand	Short sentences, familiar words, and simple concepts for children eager to read on their own but still need help.